Possibilities Realized

Presented by: Becky V Baldwin

Published by Write the Book Now, an imprint of Perfect Time SHP LLC.

ISBN: 9781732989559

Table of Contents

DEDICATION

First and foremost, I dedicate this book to my Lord and Savior, Jesus Christ. If it wasn't for His spirit living in each of us nothing could ever be conquered or realized possible.

To my mom, Patricia Vannison, whose strength, encouragement and love has powered my life and goals to be all I desire to be because I was created for greatness.

Lastly, to my daughter, Lauren Nicole. Her existence and unconditional love have always fueled the fire deep within me to live my life as an example of the heritage of strong women we derive from. Those who planted the seeds in me to help her manifest the seeds that was planted in her through our generational connection.

Love, Becky

FOREWORD

Possibilities Realized is a collection of real, raw, and inspiring stories that are a true testimony to the triumphant power of the human spirit. It has been said that it is not the challenges we encounter upon life's journey that define us, but how we respond to those challenges. In this collection of short stories, each contributing author tells a poignant story in which they unselfishly share with the reader a challenging aspect of their life that could have ruined them in mind, body, or spirit, yet they fought the good fight and prevailed to be an inspiration to others.

These authors have given us a gift—a bird's-eye view into an aspect of their life from which we can learn without having had the experience. In these authors we see a little bit of each of us or someone close to us. Yet, we learn that their experiences like our experiences need not define us. The moral of this book is, 'your dreams are attainable, if you are willing to fight for them.'.

Becky V Baldwin's vision for this book is made plain as each story unfolds. You are invited to tap into your inner strength, go after what you desire, and be encouraged that your Possibilities can be Realized!

Taren McCombs

Natosha Simpson

CHAPTER 1

Ready To Die?

By Natosha Simpson

Of all the many times in my life that I contemplated and even made attempts to take my life; I was ten years old the first time I wanted to die. So much has happened to me since then. The pain was unbearable. I felt like I was a mistake and I should have never been born. I had rough times before and after but this particular time was different.

In late April 1995 I woke up in a hospital room, feeling groggy and disoriented. My mouth tasted awful and there was black stuff on my pillow. I blinked a few times to gain focus. I quickly realized where I was in this all too familiar place. Not the regular hospital, but the one they lock us "crazies" in when they don't know what else to do with us. Once again, I had failed, I can't even overdose the right way. I survived yet again. Nineteen years old and still can't get it right. How hard could it be to die? People do it all the time every day, every minute, and every second of each day.

There was a knock at the door immediately after the door opened. "Good morning Natosha. My name is Doctor Shaw. Can you state your first and last name for me?"

"You just called my name."

"I know its protocol."

"Natosha Covington and I don't want to talk to anyone. "

"Can I just ask you a question?" I see you have been here for almost twenty-four hours and you refuse to eat or communicate with anyone. By refusing to eat, drink fluids and participate in group sessions or activities will delay your progress towards discharge. Would you like to go home in a few days?"

"Yes."

"Well do you know that cannot happen unless we are sure that you will not harm yourself?"

I chuckled at the thought. Doesn't she know that I am nothing more than a failure? All those pills I took and I am still here.

"Doctor it's not me that you need to worry about. My attempt was unsuccessful as you can see, so I have decided to change my plan. I will reign like the fires of hell on this world and spit in its face. When I am done I know for sure my life He will take."

"Natosha I am sorry, please excuse my ignorance, but I don't quite understand."

"Doctor do you believe that hell exists?"

"Not sure."

"I can confirm for you its authenticity."

"How?"

"I live it each and every day. You can't help me. If there was any help or mercy at all for me I would be dead already. There is no other way to escape my pain. My stay here will not be long."

"Why do you say that?"

"I have welfare insurance it will only cover a three day stay."

"What are your plans once you are discharged?"

"No point in making plans when you fail at everything; you just drift through life until you can no longer take it anymore then you try to end it all. Please leave me alone I want to be by myself."

"Natosha I will return in a few hours. Dinner is almost over if you would like something to eat there are drinks and snacks at the nurse's station. Hopefully, we can talk later I really would like to help you."

"No one wants to help me and no one understands."

"I believe I understand."

"No ma'am! Trust me you do not understand."

"I could have a better understanding if you would allow me to help you."

"Help me! You stand here with your fancy clothes and medical degree. I guarantee there is no way you can help me. We come from two totally different places. I live a life of confusion, endless pain and despair. I go unnoticed and I'm ignored. How can people see you every day and not know that you are miserable? Have I become so good at faking my feelings? Or has everyone around me has gotten so used to me being so pitiful that it has become the norm?" (She stood there staring at me. My heart was racing as I fought to contain the anger rising inside.)

"My anger is ready to shout, get the hell out. Leave me alone YOU cannot help me."

"There is no reason to be rude."

"You haven't seen anything yet. Huh rude is actually a compliment. So before we get too ugly and you call the code and your soldiers march in here to give me a shot, I want to be left alone. This is your last chance, goodbye."

"I will return later Natosha." Your anger doesn't frighten me and I still want to help you. I will pray for you."

"Hahahah! That's funny, no need my granny has that covered Doc you can pray for someone else, and God is tired of hearing about me. Can't you see He is so disgusted by me, that He won't even allow me to come home. My grandmother says, our home is in heaven. It doesn't seem as though I am welcomed. Please don't waste not one breath praying for me and don't come back I have nothing else to say."

I sat with my thoughts and tears. Finally at some point I fell asleep. I woke up in a panic. My head was spinning, and my heart was beating fast. I sat there just staring at the wall with tears flooding my face.

Dr. Shaw returned a few hours later.

"Natosha what's wrong?"

"Nothing!"

"That can't be true you are crying and shaking."

"How about you take a nice hot shower and put on some clean clothes it may help you feel better. I will give you a few minutes, and then I will come back. Also I have something for you.

"Ok"

When Dr. Shaw returned she had a sandwich and soda in her hand. I asked her if she lived here. She smiled and said no, why do you ask? I said it seems like you have been here for days.

We work really long shifts and someone called out tonight so I am here. I was hoping to talk to you before I left.

Why is talking to me so important to you?

I told you I genuinely want to help you.

No one has ever really wanted to help me. People say that they want to help me, but they don't mean it. Usually when I come here the doctor's come in ask a few questions then write orders for meds. Just drug me up and send me home in three days. It's bad enough being here. Whether I am in here or out there no one really cares. People have done whatever they wanted to me and no one ever said, I'm sorry. There are some people that I never want to say they are sorry. It will not count for anything coming from them. The damage is too significant. The things they did to me killed me on the inside. My mother never stood up for me and she never said she was sorry. When kids would bully me in school she would say, you better get your ass out there and fight back. She used to lock me out the house until I would fight back. I didn't want to fight.

Dr. Shaw was different she fought to keep her emotions in check as she said thank you for opening up. Would you like to continue talking? No, is that a sandwich for me? Dr. Shaw smiled and responded yes it is. I will let you eat and then I will return. You can stay, you are a lot different since we last spoke. What changed? I had a really bad dream. Do you want to talk about it? No. Ok is there anything else you want to talk about? No but thanks for the food. You are welcome. Group will be starting in a few minutes I hope you will join us.

On my way to group I noticed a white board hanging behind the nurse's station. On it was a category list one column was labeled detox and underneath was my name. They think I am an addict. I sat in the group looking and listening. Many people sat around in a circle and took turns talking. I was uncomfortable, but I sat there listening and wondering why I was on the detox unit.

After group Dr. Shaw and I talked a little more. I asked her why I was on the detox unit and she explained that it was a precaution as the admitting doctor was not sure if the over dose was intentional or not. I told her that I had been hospitalized several times and never opened up to anyone. She was different. Although I did not want to admit it I believed that she was sincere. I also appreciated that she did not drug me up and leave me somewhere staring out a window. She asked about the dream again.

Natosha can you tell me what you dreamed about that had you so upset? I dreamt that she wouldn't make it. She was drifting through life never smiling and too afraid to take her own life. She was standing on a bridge and I was calling her name, but she couldn't hear me. She will not make it without me.

Who is she?

My twin sister.

Must be exciting having a twin.

Yes sometimes. Other times it's hard because her mother favors her.

"You mean your mother."

I don't have a mother.

She looks like her more than I do and they are like besties. I feel like an outcast and I got tired of trying to fit in. So I don't care anymore. They say I have a very nasty attitude and maybe I do. I earned it.

"Natosha, I am sorry that you feel that way and for all that you've been through."

"Doctor what is wrong with me?"

"You are clinically depressed and experiencing suicidal and homicidal ideation. I believe that you may also have a chemical imbalance. I will need to run some tests."

"OK."

"I would like for you to stay here for a while. Don't worry about the insurance. I would like you to help me create a treatment plan for you. In the meantime attend some more group sessions. Then after you are discharged you can continue group therapy in outpatient services."

"How long do I have to stay and will I see you in outpatient services?"

"We can take it one day at a time. You will see a therapist in outpatient, but I will check in and you can call me if you want to talk. You may have to leave a message, but I will call you back. If there is anything that is not working well for you in outpatient we can change the program. You can also request a different therapist. I think it's great that you have a twin and you want to be here for her. My goal is to get you healthy so that you want to be here for yourself as well."

"Thanks Dr. Shaw."

She gave me a quick embrace and told me to get some rest.

Life is not easy and mental health is very real. In spite of what I have been through I have learned that I have a purpose. Overcoming my pain was a process that I had to commit to. That process continues today. After all my trials and tribulations I have realized anything is possible and the possibilities are endless.

I Thank God for my life and the blessing of livIng it.

Every attempt to commit suicide is a cry for help. Every successful attempt is a cry that went unheard or unnoticed.

Thank you for your support!

Becky Baldwin

Xavier Simpson

Krystal Simpson

Dezmen Covington

Renee McMahon

Tanneesha Covington

Michelle Simpson

Robin Espy-Harlan

Chris Harrod

Sonya Smith

About Natosha Simpson

Natosha Covington was born and raised in Pittsburgh Pennsylvania. She has lived in the Washington DC area (DMV) for about 17 years. She has a 16 year old son who she absolutely adores. Truth of the matter is he saved her life, but he doesn't really know that yet. Natosha married Xavier Simpson six years ago and is now Natosha Simpson. She now has one biological child and five beautiful step-children.

She works in the nonprofit sector and has done so for the last 20 years. She is very passionate about helping people, especially vulnerable people, who cannot help themselves.

Natosha who once believed that she was worthless and should have never been born, now realizes that there is a purpose for her life. More so a plan that may justify all the pain she endured. Having just recently realized that she is unstoppable.

She is dedicated to pursuing a dream that she once thought had died inside. This dream now reborn will cultivate an unsuspecting audience.

Yolanda Andrews

CHAPTER 2

Angels Chose Me

By Yolanda Andrews

Why was I chosen by Angels to be raised? Was it my curly hair? Was it my beautiful smile? Was it my plump cheeks, or was it they felt sorry for me, because I was abandoned? I know the answer! My Angels were sent by God to give me the perfect life, I would have never had! You see, I was adopted by Sallie and James Andrews, my mom and dad. Despite them not being my biological parents, they were truly my God sent parents! I could have never asked for better parents, if I had hand picked them myself!

One love, one mother, one father and six kids equal my family! I was the fifth child out of six children raised by my parents. This family was chosen specifically for me! How fortunate were we, just one big happy family, regardless of how we were blended together! For much is not known to me about my birth and the months to follow. What had been revealed to me when I was older was that I had been in a foster home prior to social service placing me in the care of my Godly Angels. I was only sixteen months, unaware of how my life would unfold and come to be.

According to my court records, my birth mother terminated her parental rights on June 17, 1966. The earliest photo that I have of myself, I'm almost two years old. In my mind, I was never troubled because my parents were who God had birthed for me. I've never had any desire to want to look for my birth parents, not even once! My life as a child was just that spectacular!

Fast forward to 1981, I'm sixteen and a sophomore in high school. This was a prime time in my life because I was taking driver's education and was soon to be driving! After passing that class, I couldn't wait to get my learner's permit. It was about to happen, I was going to be considered grown in my own eyes! When I asked my mom for my birth certificate, this is when my being adopted became real for me for the first time in my life! My mom only had the court order adoption paperwork and never had a birth certificate for me all these years! What was I to do now? My excitement for passing my drivers exams deflated for a minute, as I now had to tackle a hurdle I had never thought about.

In their amazing way, my parents assured me everything would work out and that I would get my learners permit! So I took to pen and paper and wrote a letter to the Maryland Department of Vital Statistics to request a copy of my birth certificate. Well three weeks passed and an official letter came addressed in the mail to me. Yes, it was my birth certificate and I was nervous!

Oh my goodness, this was the first glimpse of who I really was when I came into this world. I remember the anxiety of not knowing what to expect, as I opened the envelope and began scanning my birth certificate. I saw my first name (Yolanda), my birth last name (Griffin) crossed out, but enough for me to see it, followed by my adopted last name of Andrews. I now knew the time I was born, the name of the hospital I was born in, as well as the full names, ages, city and occupations of my birth parents.

My Angel parents were right, everything worked out and I received my learner's permit. My mom placed my birth certificate in the family bible, where it remained until I applied for my passport. No additional hiccups occurred during my teenage years, thank God.

In October 1986, I conceived my first of two children. My beautiful daughter, Kelsey, was born. I remember the overwhelming feeling of becoming a mother. The feeling of seeing my first born was one of the many treasured moments in my life. She was beautiful and I fell in love with her at first sight.

It was a normal day in May of 1987 and Kelsey was seven months. Up until this moment everything was perfect and I was on the top of the world! This would be the day that would forever change my world, leaving me full of fear! I was in the kitchen making bottles and Kelsey was in her bouncy seat. I was talking in baby jargon, to her when I noticed she wasn't responding in her baby talk, as she normally did! You see, when I was speaking to Kelsey my face was not visible to her during our exchange. I immediately picked up the phone and called my mom and told her that Kelsey was not responding when I was talking to her. My mom thought everything was probably fine, but suggested that I come over to her house.

My mother had a collection of bells on her room divider that separated the dining room from the living room. I sat my daughter in the living room facing the big window with her back towards us. We each took a bell and in synchronized fashion, rang them! To my dismay Kelsey did not respond, or flinch to the sound! I was devastated and began crying! My mom comforted me the best she could and reassured me that all would be fine and I believed her! I recall wishing my dad was there! Unfortunately, my father had passed away in 1983.

After being evaluated, Kelsey was diagnosed with a bilateral sensorial hearing loss, moderate to severe. As new young parents this was unknown territory! I recall having a dozen of questions for the pediatrician. Dr. Bold answered all of our questions and ordered more tests. Dr. Bold made the appropriate referrals for Kelsey to receive services from the county. Prior to us leaving Dr. Bold's office, he offered me praise for detecting Kelsey hearing loss early! He assured me that because of my awareness to act quickly, it would ultimately help Kelsey in the long run.

In the beginning, there was not an explanation as to the etiology of Kelsey's hearing loss. However, we would learn later that her hearing loss was present at birth! I took stock of that moment and felt that I had failed Kelsey somehow! Was it my fault? My husband's maternal/paternal family history was ruled out, so that just left me! The unknown was terrifying! I would go on for years carrying this burden of guilt.

Dr. Bold, Kelsey's pediatrician was correct in his counsel that my early detection would help Kelsey in the long run! We would witness all of her achievements in school from the early days in the infant-toddler program, grade school, high school and even college!

By October 1993, I was pregnant with my second child. At that moment, I became cognitive of the fact that I now needed to know my biological medical history for my family's sake! In July 1994, I gave birth to my second child Nick. He was healthy, happy and adorable. His hearing was checked within the first six weeks of birth and no hearing loss was detected. Thank you Jesus!

On two separate occasions in the year of 2000 and 2002, I contacted the Maryland Department of Human Services, to register for the Mutual Consent Registry and Adoption Search Services to seek medical information. Each time I had completed the paperwork sent but would never mail them back! In May of 2003, tragedy struck our family. My sister passed from cancer. Our family suffered a great loss. This was a devastating time in my life and the effects of her passing still resonate today. There is not a day that goes by that I am not reminded just how much I miss her. Losing her fueled that light within me to try again to find my medical history.

In July of 2004, I paid for an online search query using my birth mother's name. The search came back with possible addresses and phone numbers. There were two addresses listed that were literally five and twenty minutes from where I grew up my whole life. I again stop short of following through!

In the summer of 2008, four months after my mother's passing, I decided that it was now or never! So I left work early and drove to one of the addresses I had obtained from the online search, years prior! Boy was I nervous! I remember rehearsing what I wanted to say multiple times. After sitting in my car for about 15 minutes, I finally got out and knocked on the door! A young lady answered the door and I paused for a few minutes, after collecting myself and I asked for my birth mother by name. The young lady told me that she did not live there, but the woman was her grandmother. She offered me her telephone number. Wow, that caught me off guard, too! I walked back to my car, feeling somewhat dejected! After I pulled myself together, I dialed the number slowly. A woman's voice answered the phone.

I started the conversation, as I had rehearsed it. I asked her several questions which she answered all yes to. She even inquired if my birth father had put me up to calling her. After explaining I was in search of medical information only and meant her no harm, the conversation took an abrupt change in her tone of voice. She stated that she had not given up a child in 1965 and vocalized some other unpleasant comments. I thanked her for her time and told her to have a nice day. I knew in my heart that she was in fact my birth mother and for whatever reason she was denying me! It was a crushing blow!

In the summer of 2011, the truth of my existence would clash with my birth mother's continued denial of me. I had learned of an incident that would cause great harm to come to my family. There was no more hiding the truth as far as I was concerned and she left me no choice, I had to make contact with my biological siblings to reveal who I was. I will admit that I was nervous as hell to meet with them. They were basically strangers to me. When we met, there was no denying that we were related, we all looked alike. I was surprised to learn that over a span of some 30 years, I had actually come into contact with several of my biological siblings and had no idea. My birth mother did have nine children as was stated on my birth certificate, but those were the children she kept! I was actually baby number 11, not 10 ! The first child she gave up was born a year before me in 1964 and the babies that soon followed each year thereafter, she terminated her parental rights. Although, I did not get to meet all of my biological siblings that day, I was able to ask them about our biological family medical history. I am at peace with my life's truths!

Adoption is not something that should be kept a secret or to be ashamed of. I have always known that I was adopted and it never bothered me because I was so loved! Angels Chose Me and I am forever proud and honored to call these two Angels my parents and my blessing. Thank you, Mommy and Daddy. I love you!

About Yolanda Andrews

Yolanda Andrews is a strong, independent, self-motivated and passionate woman who loves to give to her family, friends and help others. She is an impactful force behind the scene in making things happen. She is a proud mother of two wonderful children and the best nana to two adorable grandsons. She was adopted by two of the most wonderful Angels, her parents, that God could have created for her.

It would be an unexpected life changing event that would ignite the flame in her to search for her medical/background information. She is a strong advocate for open record access for adopted children.

Malik Hairston

CHAPTER 3

Why Stop Now?

By Malik Hairston

Funny, I used to ask myself why good things happened in my life until I was asked one day, "Why wouldn't they?" You see I'm the youngest of four sons, but the only one raised by my single father in Washington D.C. I don't know what high school was like for you, but in D.C. I witnessed my classmates and friends get locked up, or killed before the ages of 18-21. One minute you would see them in class, then the next minute you saw them on a T-shirt, saying, "R.I.P." Often I thought that would be me.

Even as I lived a decent life, trying desperately not to be influenced by peers; the odds appeared to be against me surviving, to live a normal and productive life! I do know that if it wasn't for God, my father being hard on me and having a huge family to help raise me, my vision for a future may have been hopeless! You know the saying; *it takes a village to raise a child*, I think it's especially true for a young black male in today's society.

Despite what my thoughts may have been for my future, me not succeeding in life was never an option from my family. For my father was the eighth of ten children born to my grandmother Betty J. Hairston, who has been very instrumental in my relationship with God and my grandfather Frederick O. Hairston, Sr., who was a true handcraft man. According to family, if my grandfather was given an idea about a furniture design by individuals, he would create it by hand and bring their designs to life! Unfortunately for me, my grandfather passed before I was born, but it appears that his ability to bring individuals visions to life still lives within me!

As far as my parents, they were both hard workers and my resilient father has always instilled in me to be a "go-getter"; despite him not pursuing his life dream as an artist. My mother was amazing at her craft at being a beautician! She worked at nearly every hair salon in D.C. and her work was known around the area. Though both of my parents would tell me, "Do something with your hands", I still didn't know my purpose in life as I was entering adulthood. However, I think everyone except me knew that I was destined to create and build something with my hands.

Most of my younger life, including high school, was a blur to me at times. My senior year was the first step into my journey discovering design. Being a creative kid, I just always felt the need to bring ideas to life. I didn't necessarily like art, painting, ceramics or stuff like that. I was more interested in the concept of creating ; seeing something in my head and bringing it to life. Aside from drawing, I was more attached to details and how things were made.

While in high school one of my older brothers; Dre, introduced me to design. My main source of design knowledge came from messing around in Photoshop making cover art for friends and my one graphic design class. I don't remember much from that class aside from the teacher mentioning we would learn to make T-shirts. It was like nothing else in the curriculum mattered to me, but that!

Towards the end of high school, I always thought of going to college since I was actually graduating, but it was never high on my radar. Aside from the fact that many of my family members had college degrees and my school made it a priority to get three acceptances before graduating, those were the extent of my thoughts of attending! My initial choice after high school was to attend an Art Institute until I was accepted to Hanover College in Indiana.

Listen, I had never been on a plane before and I had no idea what it would entail to be five hundred and seventy-seven miles away from home! All I knew was there was art there and It was something different to experience! Sounds harsh, I know! Let me be honest, I was a little nervous at the time and some of my family even questioned why I was going so far away. However, after talking to my oldest brother Tony, he embraced my opportunity and encouraged me to try something new!

Boy was I disappointed to discover as a freshman design wasn't even an option as a major. I had to major in Studio Art, and the only knowledge of art I had was that I knew I could draw. I recall as time progressed in college, I was ashamed to even tell people I was an art major. Having already felt the pressure of being one of the few black students on a predominantly white campus, but an art major too? It was embarrassing! I learned quickly of social constructs and how I was viewed in them. Talk about feeling like a walking tourist attraction at times. While others embraced my creativity in certain settings, I couldn't help but become self-conscious of myself. Hearing things such as "art isn't a major", having it vandalized on the walls in the art building, and constantly being haunted by the "what are you going to do with that degree" question during conversations about my major and post-graduation, was disturbing, to say the least! It was almost as if my journey was a joke! Until I enrolled in the first ever graphic design course offered my sophomore year!

Rick was the professor and mentor when it came to designing. He was someone to look up to while away from home. He was the first professor who I found at Hanover that I felt cared for me as a student and person. I remember one summer I didn't go home. It was the last summer before my senior year. I stayed in Indiana to work alongside Rick as a junior designer for my business program.

My first major project was to design the schools academic catalog: the cover and inside layout. The catalog would be seen by the entire campus and more. Yeah, it was a big deal! I learned a lot about being an actual graphic designer that summer, as well as business and a lot more about myself in general.

That summer my passion for design revealed itself when I knew I was spending long hours in the studio. After work, I would go to the art studio to design for my own purpose. I was a part of an art collective of a few artists and musicians, who I met online. I stayed in the studio so long I became cool with the custodian lady. She let me stay as long as I wanted just to create. I would be there some nights until 3 am, before biking back to the apartment off campus.

Before graduation, I knew I wanted to have a major impact with my designs and have the school involved as a whole. The catalog book was the push I needed to believe I could design anything! I wanted to design a shirt to get into the school's store! I had this real crazy panther idea that I knew would sell because it was completely different than what the school offered. However, the lady who approves what is sold in the book store did not approve it! That did not deter me though, for I was determined to have the students on this campus see my design. I just didn't know how.

Then an opportunity came to design for a campus event called *Unity Fest*. They had a design contest for someone to create the logo and I saw this as my opportunity to get my design seen, even if it was just by a few. Guess whose design was selected out of all the entrees? Yep, mine! It blew my mind to see 400 plus students on campus, receiving my shirt that day! I was blown away at how God had shown up for me, I certainly wasn't expecting that! It was just one of the few things that helped me see that I was beginning to live my possibilities *unrealized*!

This same year I was awarded the most distinguished title at the president honors ceremony of my major. Unfortunately, I could not show up to receive it as I was in the studio working on my thesis. I was also a featured artist at the Art on Main for black history where I showcased black and white photography focused around social justice featuring poetry from a friend that was incarcerated. My purpose was to change the stigma of inmates, while also giving my homie hope as he faced his sentence. This was my first art show and at this moment I could honestly say I felt like an artist, not because of the show, but the message I wanted to convey was received.

After graduating from college in 2017, I went back home. At this point, I realized I left as a child with no real purpose and came back as a young man with my possibilities being revealed, yet not truly defined! This same year I had two art shows, I was looking for a job. Not receiving calls back, I found myself feeling like I was on the edge of a cliff. Dramatic I know but the feeling was very real! I contemplated if my dream was even worth pursuing if I couldn't do something as simple as obtaining a job!

I recall myself wanting to crash into a wall while driving because of the pressure of being jobless, living back under my father's roof and not having a direction in life. It didn't make sense, that I had completed four years in college to be right back where I started from! It certainly wasn't funny how I had once felt I was starting to live out my dreams, to not wanting to live at all! Despite it all, even through those dark thoughts, I could always count on a sketchbook and my laptop to make me feel at home!

Once I finally began believing in myself, despite what life may have presented me at times, I began working as a freelance designer, for brands such as; EAT, Damaged Crown, Michalee, ThinkOver Overkill, Everything202, Kicknosis and more! It was working with all these people that I can definitely say that gave me fuel to keep creating.

As a young black artist, at the age of twenty-three, I have acquired two art exhibitions advocating for social justice. I have now designed clothes worn by WNBA and NBA players. My artwork has been sold in the United Kingdom, been seen in galleries, been included in publications such as The RoundABout paper, Madison Courier newspaper, NAPIZUM Magazine and on this book cover. I am the designer for the cover of this book and now a bestselling author! I currently refer to myself as an ARTreprenuer; using creativity as the driving force for problem-solving to bring my clients dreams to life!

While this is the conclusion of this chapter, it's the beginning of new possibilities realized; for my opportunities remain endless at this point! Opportunities I made from obstacles that I will continue to face. Finding design as my passion, has taught me there's beauty in my struggles! Having worked with multiple entrepreneurs, small businesses, celebrities and even the Visionary of this book, there's something about the stressful process that makes the ending just that more rewarding! All these opportunities allowed me to appreciate that moment called "success"! These processes helped me appreciate the moments more when my clients have said, "Wow you really brought my vision to life!"

If I couldn't recall where I used to be, my possibilities would not be realized, as being a designer wouldn't mean as much to me, as it certainly does right now!

Thank you for your support!

God

Frederick Hairston Jr

Delia Nicole Clark

My 3 Older Brothers

Twilah Hairston Anthony

Family & Friends

Rick Lostutter

Cache Williams

My Midwest Homies

Becky V Baldwin

About Malik Hairston

A designer from Washington DC, formally known as **Malik Hairston** was raised by his resilient hardworking father as a "go-getter". Coming from a family of tradesmen, growing up, he was continuously told "do something with your hands".

Searching for a need of purpose, Malik realized his potential when he familiarized himself with designing and the connection with others that came with it. Living by the quote "obstacles equal opportunities," he saw a need for change in himself and his career path outside his family ties.

In a matter of two years, Malik has acquired two art exhibitions advocating for social justice. His work has been included publications such as The RoundABout paper, Madison Courier newspaper and NAPIZUM Magazine. His work has been seen in galleries, made its way to the United Kingdom and has been worn by professional athletes such as Otto Porter and NatashaCloud.

He refers to himself as an ARTreprenuer; using creativity as the driving force for problem-solving. His goal is to help people realize that there is no such thing as a dream if you have the choice to make it a reality.

"We design our own life with this thing called "choice." We're all facing obstacles every day, but it's our choice to decide if those obstacles can be turned into opportunities.

Michele D. Simpson

CHAPTER 4

Grown-*Ish*

By Michele D. Simpson

Vacation, a treasured thought. A privilege in reality. A way to escape and be vacant from daily activities...a must for the young and old at heart. Vacations also serve as respite from the bad stress at home. The chance to embark on journeys while being fearless, outside of living life in general. It is also the ability to hit the reset button, knowing that business you left behind will not be business as usual upon return. The objective is to return refreshed with new insight and prospective. It is the ultimate journey to conquering...YOU!

I can honestly say that I've truly tested the waters in my fear from taking a fast train to Florence, Italy while looking out at the Tuscany landscapes. I knew at that point that I've changed. Changed in the sense that I disallowed decisions from keeping me from the much needed vacation and knowing trepidation was at the forefront. We all have good intentions in traveling with family and friends, especially when we have done it in the past. But what happens when the plans of others have changed? …Here's the bad stress settling in. You must decide if you want to stay back to be supportive of a friend or family member, or embark on your journey? Many of us would stay and be supportive, but deep down inside, you know there is more to it. Do you measure and evaluate the impact? Should one compromise the relationship pillar of loyalty? It's pretty black and white. Decision made! You plan to stay and support. However, it is all good until the most life changing moment of traveling with others is now downgraded to an intention of selfishness. Your travel companion simply cannot go. But wouldn't mind if you could stay. The area's becoming very gray when you choose to go in another direction. The direction that will now impact your relationship. So the decision was made and you stuck to the original plan...EUROPE—'here I come'... *ALONE!?!* The facts were not compelling enough for me to stay OR instead of staying....to miss another adventure filled with new excitement and discovery, but you are ready to make your scrapbook memories.

Depending where you are in your life journey, you have to determine your level of comfort in all life's circumstances. I have been tremendously humbled by this experience and have taught myself to be brave enough to travel abroad alone. I left my greatest responsibilities: being a single parent, head of household and boss. I have had time to think, relax and plan my next move in life - with the unfortunate understanding that it would have to be without friends that were dear to my heart. I have truly tested my anxiety and pushed the ends of my limits. As a result, I discovered an inner bravery that I would not have seen without taking this trip alone. I hope that this message will encourage anyone to be brave and not let others' life experiences hold them back.

But it does not only stop there. This story of my traveling decision stemmed from other life areas and choices in my life specifically from the past. I tried to analyze exactly how I got here. It can truly take one testimony, one story to change your perspective in life and contextually apply the same concept to other areas of your life. With the combination of growing in your spirituality, applying pressure to the very things in your life that makes you uncomfortable may perhaps help you reach your triumph of being GROWN in 2019 and beyond.

The "little girl" in Us

Most of us, as women, have been delighted in receiving childhood guidance on how to be an adult through the lens of the experienced. It's been the influence of the near and dear to our hearts; perhaps our mothers, grandmothers, sisters, aunties, cousins and family friends. That lens becomes magnified over time making situations much larger and complicated. These figures often teach us how we should conduct ourselves from an early age in order to mold us into the young ladies we are destined to be. This is in the way we talk to others, conduct ourselves in various situations and how we value ourselves within society. I was always a person that wanted to please people, even if it meant to be at my own sacrifice. I wanted to be accepted by all, but only succeeded by most. If it meant fitting in, why not? I just wanted to be accepted. What time taught me, is that people will not always love you, but you have to find the root as to why you need that much acceptance in the first place.

In my quest to figure things out, I certainly learned that I was merely trying too hard and that my self-esteem was so low that I was willing to please others at my own cost. At this detriment, it was demonstrated by using my resources financially, agreeing to things that did not necessarily line up with my values and most importantly, not saying, "NO!" I was so utterly disappointed in the amount of time and energy I had expended, all for it not to yield the results of true friendship. The experience taught me that sometimes, no matter how hard I try, people are only around for the purposes of finding out what they could extract from me. My unbalanced selfless behavior had proved toxic to my being. It had ran its course, and I had to re-route.

The Journey to *Real* Adulthood

Looking back on my journey to adulthood, I would say overall that it was rewarding. I owned my own home, married, raising my little boy and successfully working in a non-profit organization that helps other people. I felt based on my chronological age, that I was "GROWN." I worked very hard to establish a lifestyle that I could live with. I wanted to believe that I had full control in knowing how to conduct myself, hold others accountable and be very specific in what I was willing to do for others. I enjoyed helping people--

STILL. It was my true passion; after all, I didn't think I was that vulnerable anymore.

Work was busy and expectations were high. I finally had a job where I made the most money I ever made. I got promoted! You couldn't tell me *anything*. After all, they had the best! Although everything seemed great, I lacked motivation. I was working too hard and wearing thinner by the day. Coming home late, attempting to keep up with the over 100 emails I received daily slowly began to make me lose myself. I remembered one evening coming home and feeling as if I were going to have a heart attack. I had trouble sleeping, I was eating unhealthy foods at different times of the day and replaying my entire day when it was time to rest. I was doing entirely too much and not saying, "No" enough. I was superwoman. I did not know how to take off the cape. Once again, proving to those that needed to know that I was more than capable to get the work done. IT STILL WAS NOT GOOD ENOUGH. I lost that job. One of my greatest defeats ever. I had forgiven myself, ask God's forgiveness and focus on what was really important. I had to see the possibility of knowing I was God's child...REALIZED! He ordered my steps very carefully and I found myself back on the right path. My growth in my spirituality paved the way from that storm to the many storms ahead. I now had armor to fight.

As life started getting stable, my personal life started to take its toll. During my time of unemployment, I was simply hoping to get the level of support from my life partner to keep afloat. My marriage was strangling me because I always said, "Yes" and reciprocity was non-existent. This was yet again me doing absolutely too much. I can honestly say, I didn't ask for much, but a few basic assurances. Slowly but *unfortunately* surely, we were slipping away. Possibility of becoming a single parent...REALIZED!

The "GROWING" Part Got Easier

There should be something that I acknowledge. I did in fact, cultivate a sisterhood and friendship with someone that mirrored the same level of expectation and energy I expelled. She taught me that you can still show up the same way for most, but it should be earned and not expected. You have to demand respect and assess a person's intention before doing too much. She also taught that you can still be giving of yourself in such a way that you do not lose yourself. I was finally onto something. My friendship and sisterhood with this special person taught a lifelong lesson of fellowship and honor. I no longer needed to have power struggles with people. It was time to make my circles smaller. It was a tremendous relief and we were able to complement each other in ways that strengthen our friendship and sisterhood. It is a new way of accepting people and learning more about myself. That empowerment and transferable knowledge moved in me and helped me realize the POSSIBILITY that I could surround myself around the right people who were equally motivated to have great friendships or relationships!

The possibility of being GROWN and in control was realized and it comes with responsibility and patience. I no longer needed to be the sacrificial lamb to others. I can only dream that I can pass this new trait and understanding onto my son and others with true insight, courage and wisdom to be great. Each one teach one, be accountable on how your message impacts others, be genuine on how you deliver your kind heartedness to others, and then share the good news on happiness. These life examples not only helped me grow as a woman, but helped me reduced insanity. If we do the same thing over and over again, we will get the same result. If we are patient, then the possibility is endless.

I no longer need to act as others would expect me to. I no longer need to struggle with people. I no longer need to fit in…because the truth of the matter, you have to become a better you. Through the many friendships, relationships and life experiences that I had with people, the constant theme I kept going was what I was willing to do for them. When I did not offer the level of support they were expecting in me, I was dropped like a hot potato. I believed that our friendship or relationship could stand the test of time. It did not and my feelings were impacted. It all was unfortunate and I had to recoil. In a sense, I felt free and no longer obligated to please. How would that feel? Wonderful. My circles needed to get smaller as I was coming to the realization that my values were changing. Situations were no longer equitable as anticipated.

Now that my fearlessness is at center-stage in my life, understanding the GROWN woman I am does not gain me authority based on my chronological age. The once selfless girl, young lady and adult I am today has cultivated into a beautiful creature that can use discernment and God's will to make good decisions. The confidence that I exude can propel in areas that will help me contribute to society in ways I could never imagine. I hope in true form that someone can benefit from my selfless act as it is my passion and mission to share this testimony with those who need to hear it the most. In existentialism theory, "What Doesn't Kill You Makes You Stronger," is a philosophy that I understand collectively. God doesn't give you more than you can handle. "Oh, you think you grown...?" Why yes! Just a little bit more than yesterday.

Thank you for your support!

Mrs. Earlene Simpson

Mrs. Natosha Simpson

Ms. Nicole Simpson

Ms. Kendra Brown

About Michele D. Simpson

Michele D. Simpson was born and raised on Long Island, New York. She has one son, Ethan. Michele is currently a Director for a non-profit organization serving men and women with intellectual and developmental disabilities. Her goal is to complete her Master's in Business Administration and become an inspirational and motivational speaker. She enjoys spending time with her son, mother, sister and best friend.

In her spare time, she enjoys interior decorating for close family and friends. It is her future passion to turn that pastime into a business. It is truly important to make a house a home and to help others enjoy the environment they live in. It is her mission to spread positivity and to challenge each and every person she has the privilege to encounter to live their best life.

MICHELE D. SIMPSON

Cheryl J. Naylor

CHAPTER 5

VISIONS

By Cheryl J. Naylor

I am the youngest of four children. I wasn't much of a talker; I'm still not. I didn't express my feelings much, and you didn't know what I was thinking, but I am a watcher. You can learn a lot just by watching. There was a story told to me by my mother about a time my grandmother was holding me as a baby. I would just blankly stare to the point my grandmother got nervous and gave me back to my mother, but not before saying "here, take this child, she is scaring me." But she also said, "this is the child who would hold the family together." My grandmother had a vision of me as she held me in her arms. My grandmother has now passed, but I always remember what my mama told me.

I've had my own visions. At the time they happened, I did not know they were visions. They were just a moment in time. When what I envisioned in my mind actually happened, it was then and only then that I knew what I saw years before was a vision. It was that moment when I knew that visions were more than daydreams, they were real. They were possibilities realized. So far, this has happened two times in my life. Let me tell you about the first vision.

Growing up tall and slim in New York City, I got involved in modeling. I modeled for non-profit organizations and local designers. In my mid-twenties, I went to Ophelia Devore School of Charm where young black women learned etiquette, poise, posture, and confidence. I loved it! I loved modeling. I loved the arts, the glitz and glamour. I went from modeling to being a part of an organization who hosted fashion shows. This one time after a fashion show, all the models and designers were in a suite at the Marriott Marquis on Broadway in New York City. I must have been about 27 years old at the time. I just so happened to look out the window, and the view from there was amazing. Looking at all the lights on Broadway with a sky-high view stopped me in my tracks. The moment was surreal. All time stood still, and I said to myself "I want that view." I woke up from that moment to continue on with a show well done.

Fast forward 14 years later, a lot has happened; marriage, divorce, short and long-term boyfriends, almost married again, and school. I was still in the midst of that 36-year journey. I then decided I wanted to leave New York. Although I was born and raised in New York, I outgrew it. New York became too expensive, too crowded, and not conducive to my lifestyle. I could not study for my classes when the guy in the house behind me wanted to be the neighborhood DJ, and he wanted to be it all night long. I also said when the rent became $1,000.00, that was a mortgage payment. Why not let it be my mortgage payment. So, I searched for employment out of state. I searched in Atlanta and Washington, DC. I would travel back and forth for interviews. Two years from beginning my search, I got a job. Woohoo! I was leaving New York known as the Big Apple and moving to Silver Spring, Maryland. I did not know much about Maryland or the Washington DC metro area, but I was going. My boyfriend at the time actually found me a two-bedroom apartment. I didn't need two bedrooms, but that is what was available. I said I can always downgrade to a one bedroom at a later time. I was stepping out on faith. Everything was done online. I did not even see the apartment until I moved in. I packed up my stuff, loaded the truck, said my goodbyes and headed south. I was so busy with the move, that I couldn't stop to think. As night fell, and I was finishing moving my things in, I just so happen to look out the window, and bam! There it was…the view; a beautiful view. A view of the White House. I froze and 14 years earlier flashed before my eyes. I said "wow". This has happened. As I stared out the window, I said, "if this can happen, then my other vision can happen too." That moment was a "possibility realized." That moment I sat in my faith and said I am going to be alright because God's got this.

This leads me to my second vision. (A party in the backyard). But not just any party, a party in the backyard of the house I will own. You see as a single mom, I was lucky to have a support system to help with my son. I had help from my sisters and my mother; I even had a babysitter. Babysitters did not charge a mortgage payment back in the early eighties. I worked hard and did what I had to do to provide for myself and my son. There were times when I would drop the baby off at the babysitter's house and go to work. I worked at a daycare center as a teacher's aide at the time. I would then go to school, go back to work, pick the baby up to start all over again the next day. I was grateful to have family there to pitch in whenever necessary. That's why when I decided that I wanted a house, it wasn't going to be just for me, it was going to be for my mother as well. Please don't discount anything that happens in your life. Everything, and I mean everything happens for a reason.

While living in New York, my girlfriend gave me a flyer for a homeownership program, which was nationwide. I attended the seminar and worked with this program with the hope that one day I would be able to buy a house. When I moved to Maryland, I continued the program in their Washington, DC location. For three years, I did everything they told me to do. I saved what I needed to save. I provided everything they needed me to provide. I was determined. As I previously said, this house wasn't just for me, it was for my mother as well for when she retired. I had to get her out of the Brownville projects. A place that was becoming less desirable with every passing year. There wasn't a time when you can get in the elevator and there wasn't piss in there. Gunshots and drugs were a norm and cops on the rooftops checking out the neighborhood from up top. Then one day as I was sitting at work, the office called me and said "the mortgage rates have dropped to a record low. Get your butt in here and fill out the mortgage application." Well maybe not the word "butt", but you get the message. That was God. He would move heaven and earth to get you what is yours, and at a low rate too. I ran quick, fast, and in a hurry, to take advantage of the low mortgage rates. I was approved. A single woman at the age of 47 doing it by herself was going to be a homeowner. I purchased my home six months later in January of 2010 and brought my mother and my uncle down to live with me. Some of my nieces with their children followed. I guess I was fulfilling my grandmother's vision of keeping the family together. That summer, I had the biggest backyard party you can imagine with family and friends.

There is power in the vision and moments of revelation. Some so brief that we miss it. Some so hard that it knocks us over. I experienced both. One in the hotel suite in the midst of a celebration and one while unpacking to start my life in a new apartment far from my New York home. Do not diminish the value of your thoughts. They can manifest the life of your dreams. The possibilities are boundless. As I am writing and telling my story to you, I am in the midst of planning a wedding; my wedding. Unlike my looking-over-the city and backyard-party visions, I did not have a previous vision for my wedding day. This vision is unfolding as I am planning. Sometimes I wish I had a prior vision. Then I could say, that's it. I know what I want. But planning a wedding at the moment is working out and creating joy just the same.

Visualize where you are and don't miss the moment of where you want to go or who you want to be. During those quiet times or even during those times when so much is going on like when the baby is crying, the house needs to be cleaned, the report was due two hours ago or traffic is a nightmare, picture in your mind all that is possible. VISUALIZE! Permeate the air with the aroma of your positive visions. Speak to the universe because it listens.

Thank you for your support!

Louis E Naylor, Jr.

Louis E Naylor III

Kadija Hunnicutt

Jeannette Pringle

Darren Washington

Angela Wooden

Cheryl Dent

Gina Sobers

Ethlyn Carroll

Justin Pringle

About Cheryl J. Naylor

Cheryl Naylor is a quiet storm, a woman of peace and perseverance, and a force to be reckoned with. She is a true example of possibilities realized, and a firm believer that God has a distinct and personal plan for her life.

Just finishing her first year of college, she found herself a single mom. Thirty-six years later, she graduated with a Bachelor of Science Degree in Psychology with a minor in Business Administration from the University of Maryland University College.

Her accomplishments and perseverance have led her to be recognized as a person of patience and faith. She is passionate about helping others achieve their goals and volunteered as an adult education teacher at the YWCA. Knowing she's played a part in the success of another is a bone-chilling joy. For more than thirty years, Cheryl has worked in the accounting field as a Client Billing Specialist for multi-million-dollar law firms.

Outside of work, she enjoys family, friends, music, and quiet mornings. It allows the mind to speak to the heart, and the universe to listen.

Becky V Baldwin

CHAPTER 6

When the Bottom Falls Out

By Becky V Baldwin

1990 our family was officially growing and we had a beautiful baby girl! At the time my husband and I were what was referred to as "yuppies" because both of us were working for two of the top companies in the District of Columbia and we were making great salaries. We were living our best life as a couple, buying homes, especially as our family structure grew. My spouse was a good provider and I lived my life free of major financial responsibilities like a mortgage, car notes, insurance, etc. I had the flexibility to shop, plan vacations and enjoy the fun of the 90's. Life appeared to be perfect!

Well, due to some seen and unforeseen events I found myself single with a 14-month old baby and no job. I was homeless, jobless and penniless. Divorce caught me by complete surprise. The surprise came because growing up I saw my great aunts and other women hold their marriages and families together through catastrophic life events, so I assumed my husband and I would also be able to work through whatever happened - nope, that wasn't my experience. I was definitely surprised! I was also afraid. I got married and left my mother's house to move in with my husband, so I had never taken care of myself and now I had to do it with a baby no less. I was in a place where I had no reference or understanding of how to move forward or how to be on my own and be responsible for everything involved with living independently. As I said, my spouse was a good provider and was great with money management…that was never my strength.

"You may feel lost and alone, but God knows exactly where you are, and He has a good plan for your life." -Daily Inspirational Quotes

Thank God for mothers. I went to live with my mom in her two bedroom apartment. My mom never judged me or made me feel like a failure ,but I felt like the biggest failure ever. Here I was without enough money to even rent an apartment or buy food. I felt as though I wasn't just a failure, but I was a SUPER failure.

My mom encouraged me because she was a single mom and as I recalled my upbringing I realized I had what it took to make it - I came from strong female women who showed me how to encourage and empower yourself to do what you have to do so you can do what you want to do!

I'd left my amazing job a week before my bottom seemed to fall out. I quit because I found out that my baby was staying with a daycare provider who didn't feed her and left her alone daily with a teenage boy managing her and the other children. My child's health and welfare was at risk, so I felt I had no other choice ,but to quit. A few days had passed and I went to a placement agency seeking work. I was unemployed, so they wanted to pay me very little. My hourly rate was cut by 80%, but I had to work because we had to live. God blessed me to work with an amazing company and every 90-days I was getting a raise. Yet, I still wasn't able to buy furniture, pay a car note, save money, etc. I decided to pursue a divorce, which led to a substantial amount of legal bills.

I lived in a friend's home in Suitland, MD for a period of time and another friend gave me furniture that she planned to replace. My pride was bruised but my spirit was not shaken, because I knew I had to do what I had to do. These amazing friends created the space and opportunity for me to get on my feet.

Over the next year I started to get my momentum to get it all done. I was starting to get my head above water, so to speak. Most of the time, I felt like I had more month than money, but thanks to God, I never lost power, had our water shut off, or have our car repossessed. I did the work and a few years later, I was able to buy a home, in Upper Marlboro, MD for me and my daughter. Guess what? In a few years, I lost my house because I lost my job, and I'd used all my savings to buy my house. Back to my mom's two bedroom apartment we went...I was back to where I had started. Now, my spirit was shaken. I started feeling sorry for myself and I couldn't seem to pray. I was angry. I was hopeless. I was depressed. I was a failure! I knew I was not like all the amazing women I'd had in my life. I wasn't strong. I wasn't capable. My mom sat me down and had a "come to Jesus moment" with me. She told me what she saw in me and that I had to get myself together for my daughter who was watching me. See now my daughter was 10 years old. I went to a hotel and spent an entire weekend. I cried. I screamed. I said negative things to me about me. I felt sorry for myself and when I was empty of feelings and I had no more tears to cry I fell to my knees and prayed.

One of the things I've learned the hard way is that it doesn't pay to get discouraged. Keeping busy and making optimism a way of life can restore your faith in yourself. -Lucille Ball

When I walked out of the hotel Sunday afternoon I felt so different. I realized how blessed I was to have my mom and great friends and an amazing daughter who believed in me. In less than three months we moved into an apartment in Bowie, MD for a year, but we needed more space so, we moved into a rented house in Temple Hills, MD that was a great distance from her school but it was closer to my daughter's gymnastic facility. My daughter was a great athlete and in under two years she was competing at a statewide level. She enjoyed gymnastics and I wanted to make sure she could continue at all costs. Well, after sprucing up the rental house with a fresh coat of paint, landscaping, and upgrading the deck, the owner decided he wanted to move back into the house.

Again, I ended up back at my mom's two bedroom apartment, but this time only for 4 weeks. I was able to find a place in Waldorf,

MD for me and my daughter to live and we did until she graduated from high school and started college.

My daughter was talking to some friends one evening when I overheard her say "I've lived in every city in Prince George's county Maryland including D.C." When I heard her say that it broke my heart because I felt I'd failed to give her the security that comes with stability. Her dad still lived in the home we moved out of 17 years earlier. I remember apologizing to her with tears running down my face. I was apologizing for moving so often and not providing her with stability and continuity. She looked at me like I'd just grown a second head and said "Ma, I never felt that way. In fact, I was bragging because I told my friends that my mom moved wherever she knew I would have a better experience." She told me, "each move was never about you. Actually each move made your drive to work longer and longer. Each move was a better place, a better school, and a better gym for me. I've had an amazing childhood and never wanted for anything."

"Our wounds are often the openings into the best and most beautiful part of us."
-David Richo

As a woman, I was busy judging myself in the eyes of those who I thought were judging me e.g., gym moms, school moms, ex-husband and myself. My daughter saw my strength and determination. She saw that nothing is impossible but everything requires work and perseverance.

We lived in five cities in Prince George's county in Maryland not to mention four times in my mom's apartment in D.C. I was worried about moving so much; but my struggles, that I felt I was not handling well, in actuality my daughter saw possibilities can be realized through me, her mom!

My ultimate surprise was to realize I was as strong as the women who raised, encouraged and inspired me all my life. I realized my family was all those amazing great aunts, mother, aunt, grandmother and great-grandmother who nurtured the spirit of faith and determination in me. I was able to keep my family together regardless of what circumstances. I realized that family is made up of those who stay the course and who never stop loving you - even when you sometimes may not be able to love yourself. I remembered that I come from an amazing strong woman and that drive lives within me and my daughter. I continue to emerge into the woman God designed me to be and I am truly blessed.

Thank you for your support!

Patricia Vannison

Lauren Baldwin

Great Aunt, Betty Mae Withers

Taren McCombs

Malik Hairston

Yolanda Andrews

Cheryl Naylor

Michele D. Simpson

Natosha Simpson

Charell Withers Cook

About Becky V Baldwin

Becky has always had a heart and willingness to serve! While attending Howard University she majored in physical therapy, but quickly found a passion for human resources. Over the last 30 years she has provided her professional expertise in various industries, but have found a home at a large social service agency handling recruitment, hiring, and training of employees that support a vulnerable population in homeless shelters, transitional housing, schools, community living facilities, and employment service programs throughout the District of Columbia.

She has also been able to further support the population by participating in hurricane and natural disaster relief efforts; serving meals and buying Christmas gifts for needy children and their families, as well as other community efforts to make a difference for those who needed it. Her desire to serve has transferred to her passion to do more personally as well as professionally by providing all natural and organic products that aid in optimum health and life performance for children, women and men; thus she has become a business owner with Total Life Changes (TLC).

As a Director and distributor with TLC, she has been blessed to share and be a part of over 100 people's decision and commitment to live a health-wealthy lifestyle – l TLC is not a medical company nor does it make claims to be, but she has been able to share her story/testimony of better health and weight loss and convinced others that good health is easy, fun and sustainable.

Becky is the founder of Emerge, Inc. an organization dedicated to lifestyle embetterment through wellness choices and a Best Seller Author in the anthology, "You Don't Know Our Stories - From Trials To Triumph.

Made in the USA
Middletown, DE
04 July 2019